BARCELONA

NANCY DUNNAN

THE
GREAT
CITIES
LIBRARY

A BLACKBIRCH PRESS BOOK

WOODBRIDGE, CONNECTICUT

Published by Blackbirch Press, Inc.
One Bradley Road, Suite 205
Woodbridge, CT 06525

Printed in Hong Kong
Bound in the United States of America

Editors: Kailyard Associates
Maps: Robert Italiano
Photo Research: Photosearch, Inc.

Library of Congress Cataloging-in-Publication Data

Dunnan, Nancy.
    Barcelona/Nancy Dunnan.
    (The Great cities library)
    Includes bibliographical references and index.
    Summary: Describes the past, the people, and the things to see in the
various sections of Barcelona, site of the 1992 Olympic games.
    ISBN 1-56711-018-5
    1. Barcelona (Spain)—Geography—Juvenile literature. [1. Barcelona
(Spain)—Description.] I. Title. II. Series: Great cities (New York, N.Y.)
DP402.B25D86 1991
946'.72—dc20   91-18904
                                                            CIP
                                                             AC

pages 4–5
The Plaza España, with Mount Tibidabo in the background.

CONTENTS

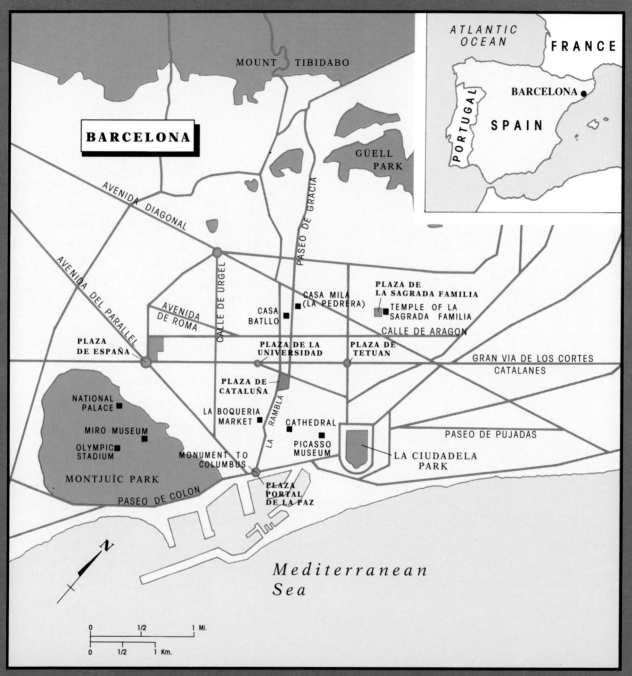

MOUNT TIBIDABO

GÜELL PARK

BARCELONA

ATLANTIC OCEAN

FRANCE

BARCELONA

PORTUGAL

SPAIN

AVENIDA DIAGONAL

AVENIDA DEL PARALLEL

PASEO DE GRACIA

AVENIDA DE ROMA

CALLE DE URGEL

CASA MILA (LA PEDRERA)

CASA BATLLO

PLAZA DE LA SAGRADA FAMILIA

TEMPLE OF LA SAGRADA FAMILIA

CALLE DE ARAGON

PLAZA DE ESPAÑA

PLAZA DE LA UNIVERSIDAD

PLAZA DE TETUAN

GRAN VIA DE LOS CORTES CATALANES

PLAZA DE CATALUÑA

LA BOQUERIA MARKET

NATIONAL PALACE

MIRO MUSEUM

OLYMPIC STADIUM

MONTJUÏC PARK

LA RAMBLA

CATHEDRAL

PICASSO MUSEUM

LA CIUDADELA PARK

PASEO DE PUJADAS

MONUMENT TO COLUMBUS

PASEO DE COLON

PLAZA PORTAL DE LA PAZ

Mediterranean Sea

N

0   1/2   1 Mi.

0   1/2   1 Km.

Each of Spain's 15 different geographic areas has its own history, its own culture, and its own sense of identity. The region of Cataluña is on the extreme northeast of the country, and Barcelona is its capital.

Population: 1.8 million; including the outlying areas (suburbs), there are approximately 4 million people. It is the second largest city in Spain. While most of the population is Catholic, the city is home to one of the largest Jewish populations in Spain, about 5,000 people.

Size: The city covers about 35 square miles.

Nickname: La Ciudad Condal—the City of a Count.

Business Activities: Barcelona has always been Spain's leading manufacturing center. Its thriving port, abundance of electric power, and long history of international trade have made it economically successful. Not surprisingly, Cataluña accounts for more than 20 percent of Spain's gross national product of $165 billion, with just 15 percent of the population of Spain.

Most jobs in Barcelona are to be found in textiles, chemicals, automobile and truck manufacturing, machinery and metals, book publishing, papermaking, food processing, optical and precision instruments, plastics, and railroad equipment. Textiles make up 67 percent of the total Spanish output; chemicals, 32 percent; paper and graphic arts, 30 percent.

Although Barcelona sells most of its products within Spain, it also exports potash, cement, chemicals, textiles, leather goods, machinery, and agricultural equipment.

Barcelona is home to more than 60 companies from all over the world. It is also the headquarters for a number of Spain's leading financial institutions; there are over 2,000 bank offices in the city. Government is also a key business, with 25 foreign chambers of commerce and 60 permanent consulates.

7

THE PLACE

"It takes all kinds of cities to make Barcelona. It takes among others a Roman city, a Gothic city, a maritime city, and a city of cosmopolitan pleasure. And the odd thing is that none of them at first sight looks particularly Spanish."

—Kenneth Tynan

The Palacio Nacional on Montjuïc

Everything about Barcelona is a contrast. Architecturally speaking, it's a combination of medieval and modern—crisscrossing narrow streets, ancient palaces, wide boulevards, and huge sports complexes. Similarly, the city is surrounded by a varied terrain of rivers and mountains.

Topography

The city of Barcelona, which hugs the Mediterranean coast, is located 330 miles northeast of Madrid in a region called Cataluña. It lies on a gentle slope of land facing southeast to the Mediterranean between the Llobregat River on the southeast and the Besos River on the northeast. The Mediterranean stretches out in front of the city. A circle of mountains, the Sierra de Collserola, runs behind the city. The tallest of these is the Tibidabo (1,745 feet), which affords the best view of the city. The name comes from the Gospel of St. Matthew, who quotes the devil as saying, "Hace omnia tibi dabo si cadens adoraberis me." ("All this I will give you if you fall down and worship me.")

At the south end of the harbor, a fortress sits atop Montjuïc, a gentle hill rising some 570 feet above the sea. The fortress once served as the city's defense post, but Montjuïc has had a varied history. In Roman times, it boasted a temple, dedicated to Jupiter, and was called Mons Jovis, the Mountain of Jupiter; in the Middle Ages, it featured a lighthouse;

A fort that once guarded the harbor sits atop Montjuïc.

in the seventeenth century, a military castle; and in the nineteenth century, a huge Jewish cemetery, from which it takes its modern name, "Mountain of the Jews." Today it is the site of a huge sports stadium, a botanical garden, various museums, and an amusement park. It is also the site of the 1992 Summer Olympics.

Climate

Between the mountains and the sea, the city enjoys a mild climate, quite logically described as "Mediterranean." It is protected from the cold winds of the north by the Collserola mountains and cooled in the summer by breezes off the sea. The city boasts 2,500 hours of sunshine a year and a winter temperature that rarely falls below 50° F.

Geography

Like any big city, Barcelona can, at first glance, look imposing. But divide it into four parts—La Rambla, the Gothic Quarter, Montjuïc, and El Ensanche—and you'll find it surprisingly easy to get your bearings.

Barcelona at present is a "closed" city and cannot grow any larger. To keep the city at its present size and maintain its stature as one of Europe's finest places to live, Barcelona is working to restore its streets, squares, parks, and buildings. Its houses and transportation system are also being upgraded.

A museum dedicated to the work of Spanish painter and sculptor Joan Miró is on Montjuïc, not far from the Olympic Stadium.

La Rambla is a wide avenue that forms the center of Barcelona. As one of Europe's most famous pedestrian malls, it is filled with an exciting variety of sights and sounds.

Colorful varieties of flowers fill a market on La Rambla.

The center of the city is La Rambla. It is a wide, tree-lined avenue that leads from the largest square and the commercial center, the Plaza de Cataluña, south to the seafront. *Rambla* means torrent in Arabic. Long ago this was actually the sandy bottom of a stream that ran outside the medieval walls of the city. Yet even back then, when it was dry, the Rambla was a busy main street in the business district, filled with shops. Around 1366, it was paved over, and at the end of the eighteenth century, trees were planted and benches were set out. Today it is one of Europe's most famous pedestrian malls.

One can buy almost anything along La Rambla, including caged songbirds.

Not far off La Rambla and near the sea, lies the *Barrio-Gótico*, or Gothic Quarter. This is the historic heart of the city—the "original" Barcelona. Its winding stone streets and ancient buildings surrounding the Gothic cathedral are a living monument to the nobility of the thirteenth and fourteenth centuries. This section sits on a gentle hill, the Mons Taber, where the ancient Iberians built their city of Laye. Much of this area remains unchanged from the thirteenth century, making it easy to forget the twentieth century exists at all. Remnants of the old city walls dating from Roman times still remain there.

Heading back toward La Rambla, due north, you'll find the new part of town: El Ensanche. When the city was ready to expand in the 1850s, the old walls were torn down and Barcelona sponsored a competition for a new street plan (*Ensanche* means extension). The winner was an engineer named Ildefona Cerda, who designed a series of elegant boulevards and squares crossed with wide avenues. The most important thoroughfares are the Avenida del Generalisimo Franco (also called the "Diagonal") and the Paseo de Gracia, the city's luxury shopping area. This is also a fashionable residential area and the site of some famous landmarks: the University of Barcelona, the Parish Church of the Conception, the Cloister, the Plaza de Toros (bullfighting ring), and the most famous unfinished architectural work, Gaudí's *Sagrada Familia,* or Holy Family Church. The building was begun in 1882, and stopped after the architect's death in 1926. It was resumed in 1940, and still continues today. Since Gaudí died leaving no plans for the church's completion, it remains one of the city's most mysterious and enchanting sites.

Beyond El Ensanche lies the old sailor's quarter, La Barceloneta. At one time, it was located outside of Barcelona's walls, but when the city kept growing, it was gobbled up in the transition. In La Barceloneta, life has always revolved around the sea. It is full of narrow streets, sailors, artisans, and restaurants

Barcelona's busy port on the Mediterranean is an important factor in Spain's economic growth.

facing the blue Mediterranean. A French engineer, Próspero de Verboom, designed this neighborhood using the most progressive urban planning ideas. The streets are laid out in a grid, unlike most of old Barcelona, and although the houses could have only one floor, each room had a window for sunlight. Verboom's height limitation was later modified so that most houses in La Barceloneta now have two floors.

Visitors walk near the site of the 1992 Summer Olympics. The Palacio Nacional is in the background.

The Port of Barcelona, once just an open area, was improved in 1474 when a *muelle,* or breakwater, was built. It was called the Muelle de Santa Creu. But the harbor as we know it today was built in the seventeenth century. Docks and special floats for oil tankers and other huge ships are busy all year round. Close to 7,000 merchant vessels arrive each year, carrying more than 18 million tons of merchandise. Some 250 shipping lines connect Barcelona with over 100 countries.

The hard-to-explain "feel" of the city, however, is its greatest asset. Like New York and Rome, Barcelona is full of sophistication and cultural dynamism. The city is impressive on many fronts: it has many outstanding Gothic and Art Nouveau buildings, excellent museums, elegant boulevards, and a great wealth of imaginative cooking. The business surrounding the 1992 Olympics has given the city an additional boost. The slogan today is "Barcelona Mes Que Mai"—"Barcelona More Than Ever."

THE
PAST

"Barcelona, depository of courtesy, shelter of strangers, hospice of the poor, homeland of the brave, vengeance of the affronted, and gracious confluence of firm friendships, unique in setting and beauty."
—**Miguel de Cervantes**

Mediterranee

An eighteenth-century view of Barcelona's harbor

The history of Barcelona reads like a juicy novel packed with conquests and compromises, revolts and revolutions. Throughout the centuries, its people made repeated attempts to be independent from Spain.

The region of Cataluña, where Barcelona is located, has always been different from the rest of the country. Because they are actually geographically closer to France, the Catalans developed their own language, and a fierce sense of pride and independence. Today, they are more apt to say they are Barcelonans than Spaniards.

Barcelona has a dramatic history that can be seen on almost every street. The Iberians, Romans, Visigoths, Moors, and Franks all left their mark.

The Early Years

The first settlement on the site that today is Barcelona was made more than 3,000 years ago by the Iberians, one of the oldest European peoples. Little is known about the Iberians except that they were an agricultural tribe from Africa.

After the Iberians, the history of Barcelona and the Catalans is a lengthy chronicle of revolts, revolutions, and waves of foreign conquerers—beginning with the Carthaginians, also from Africa. They came during the 400s B.C. in search of land. Again, this powerful group did not leave much in the way of recorded history, and we know very little about the way they lived. We do, however, have the Barca family to thank for giving the city its name. Their famous general, Hamlicar Barca, a member of Carthage's ruling family, named the ancient city "Barcino" after himself in 281 B.C. The resident Carthaginians also named the country "Spania," or "land of rabbits."

The Romans: A.D. 50-406

Next on the scene were the Romans, who wanted Spain's rich and fertile land for themselves. It took 200 years to get rid of the scattered and stubborn Carthaginian tribes. When they were driven out, the entire Iberian Peninsula came under Roman rule. For the first time, Spain and Portugal were united under one government. Today we have not only the word *Iberia* to refer to the Spanish peninsula but the Spanish word *España*, which comes from the Roman word *Hispania*.

The Romans were one of the greatest contributors to Barcelona. In the first century B.C., the city flourished as a Roman colony. It was known as "Colonia Favencia Julia Augusta Pia Barcina." Commerce grew, and a Roman code of law was established. Aqueducts, bridges, roads, and walls were built, and an efficient administration was established. The Romans gave Spain its language, Latin, from which most of the country's languages derive. The Romans also brought Spain its primary religion, Christianity.

Ataulfo, king of the Visigoths, conquered Barcelona in A.D. 415.

The Visigoths: 406-711

Just as Barcelona was gaining ground as an important port city, it was overtaken by a Germanic Christian tribe called the Visigoths. Their king, Ataulfo, captured Barcelona in 415 and made it the capital of the Visigothic Kingdom. The Visigoths ruled for the next three centuries.

While the Romans brought technology, education, and civilization to the area, the Visigoths were illiterate and more interested in war than in building. Eventually, fights among themselves and with landlords weakened the city—and the country.

The Muslims: 711-756

The Romans laid a seed, the Visigoths had let it spoil, and now the Arab Muslims saw an opportunity to let the seed grow. On a visit to Spain around 710, one Arab ruler saw such rich land in disarray that he went back to northern Africa to tell his leaders of his find. One year later, the Moors attacked, crossing the Straits of Gibralter from North Africa. They were superior fighters and they easily defeated the Visigoths. By 718, most of the country, including Barcelona, was under their rule.

It was this period that brought the most change to Barcelona. One could say the city's "melting pot" status dates from this time. Because the Moors were Muslims (followers of Islam), many people converted from Christianity.

The Moors were one of the most advanced cultures in medieval Europe. They had made great discoveries in medicine and mathematics, and under their rule, Spain became the most powerful and civilized kingdom in the Western world. The Moors brought with them a great passion for elaborate and ornate architecture. One of their most magnificent buildings was described by the American writer Washington Irving in his book *The Alhambra*.

In Barcelona, the city's people enjoyed a quiet existence; scholars discussed, artists crafted, architects built, and merchants bargained. Because the Moors were a tolerant people, they allowed Christians and Jews to live in peace. The Jewish population of Barcelona now prospered for the first time.

Unfortunately, the Moors had more of a presence in southern Spain than in the northeastern region of Cataluña, where Barcelona is located. The city eventually fell into the hands of France's Emperor Charlemagne. The French had long been interested in their next-door neighbor, and the Moors, too far away to do anything about it, had no choice but to surrender the city.

The Golden Age: Late 700s to Late 1300s

With the Muslim frontier far from its borders, Barcelona spent the 800s to 1100s being governed by a series of rulers, called counts, who kept the city independent. This long succession of rulers gave the city its nickname—"La Ciudad Condal,"—or "The City of a Count." One of the first counts, Wilfredo El Velloso (879–897) founded the dynasty of the House of Barcelona, which ruled for centuries.

By 1100, Barcelona had dominion over all of Cataluña. The population soared to 20,000 as shipyards thrived, and merchants prospered in their trade with other Mediterranean nations. This was Barcelona's "golden age."

James I, king of Aragon, established the first ruling body of governors in Barcelona.

In the thirteenth century, under James I, king of Aragon (1214–1276), the municipality of Barcelona was set up. A local ruling body called the "Consell de Cent," or "Council of 100," was also established. It consisted of leading citizens—merchants, artists, and craftsmen. They ruled a vast empire that included Sicily, Malta, Sardinia, and most of modern Greece. Their power stemmed largely from maintaining tight control of Mediterranean trade. The city wielded such power that people joked that every fish in the

Mediterranean Sea wore the red and yellow stripes of the Kingdom of Cataluña.

This golden age lasted from the twelfth century until the end of the fourteenth century, when severe plagues, a series of bank failures, and internal fighting pushed the city into a period of financial decline.

The Christian Kingdom: Late 1300s to Early 1600s

The fifteenth century was a period of economic crisis for the region. Barcelona fell under the control of King Ferdinand and Queen Isabella. Their marriage in 1469 brought together two of the strongest kingdoms—the regions of Aragon and Castile. Their goal was to unite Spain and convert the entire population back to Christianity no matter what the cost. Because of their religious fervor, they were known as the "Catholic Monarchs."

They may have unified the country, but under their rule came one of the worst institutions in modern history: The Spanish Inquisition. The Inquisition, which was a court of law, imprisoned or killed those who did not follow Catholicism. In 1492, the Catholic Monarchs gave Muslims and Jews an ultimatum: convert to Christianity or leave. Thousands elected to flee Spain rather than become Catholic. During this time, Barcelona lost the majority of its Jewish and Muslim population, which included many of its scholars and merchants.

Queen Isabella and King Ferdinand, known as the "Catholic Monarchs," financed
Christopher Columbus's voyage to the New World in 1492.

That same year marked the arrival at the Spanish court of the great adventurer Christopher Columbus. He convinced Queen Isabella to finance his expedition to explore the New World. Columbus sailed on August 3, 1492, with three ships: the *Santa Maria,* the *Pinta,* and the *Nina.* A year later, Isabella and Ferdinand received Columbus in Barcelona upon his victorious return from America. The meeting is said to have taken place in the magnificent Tinell Salon of the Royal Palace on the Plaza del Rey. Apparently, in an unprecedented move, the king and queen actually stood to greet Columbus. Soon thereafter, the Spanish court financed other explorers, including Vasco Nuñez de Balboa, Ferdinand Magellan, and Hernando de Soto.

Columbus's trip focused attention on America's natural resources. At the beginning of the sixteenth century, the first coins of pure copper were minted and new banks were formed. Barcelona gradually experienced a turnaround. The city was hurt, though, by trade routes that favored the ports in southern Spain. The cities closest to the Atlantic Ocean—Seville and Cádiz, for example—rose in importance as Barcelona's seaport declined.

Thanks to Charles V, grandson of the Catholic Monarchs, the city recovered. (Charles V was also called Holy Roman Emperor Charles V.) He arrived in 1519 and, liking what he saw, made Barcelona the capital of the Spanish Empire. During Charles's reign, Cortés landed in Mexico, Pizarro arrived in Peru, and Spain claimed most of present-day Latin America. It also claimed the southern part of the United States from Florida to California, and the Philippines. Because of its close relationship with the Crown, Barcelona flourished and was able to maintain its separate identity and language.

French Rule: 1640-1653

After such a long period of virtually independent rule, Barcelona's people were used to getting their own way. The city now boasted a very strong middle class of workers, farmers, shipbuilders, fishermen, and teachers. It is not surprising, then, that when farmworkers were told to obey a new order that they felt was harmful to their livelihood, they refused. This is what happened in 1640, and the war that followed was called the War of the Harvesters.

Meanwhile, French forces were trying to take over several of Spain's northeastern provinces. Angry at the king's new attempts to control the city, Barcelona sided with France and refused to accept the Spanish king, Philip IV, as their monarch. After beating his troops in the bloody Battle of Montjuïc, they claimed Louis XIII the new count of Barcelona. For 12 years, the city was under French rule. When Spain finally gave in to Barcelona's demands, promising Cataluña internal autonomy in 1653, the region once again returned to Spanish rule.

A Temporary End to Catalan Autonomy: The Eighteenth Century

Peace did not last for long. The War of Spanish Succession began in 1701, and it brought more trouble to the city. (A succession war is one that grows out of a dispute over who should succeed or inherit a throne.) Still not completely in agreement with Spain's present ruler—King Philip V (1700–1746)—Barcelona sided with Archduke Charles of Austria, who had established his court in the city and had promised Barcelona complete independence if he succeeded the Crown.

Unfortunately for Barcelona, he didn't. Philip V of Spain won the war and captured Barcelona in 1714, after an 11-month siege. Some 30,000 Barcelonans died during the war defending their city. To punish the Barcelonans for holding out, Philip V moved the university to Cervera and abolished the once-great kingdom of Cataluña, reducing it to provincial status, subject to the laws of the Kingdom of Castile. Still not satisfied, the king forced the evacuation of part of the city to construct, at Barcelona's expense, a massive fortress in what today is Ciudadela Park.

Unification under the Spanish flag ended up helping rather than hurting Barcelona. New trade laws allowed Barcelona's port to grow. A decree permitting freedom of trade between the port of Barcelona and America increased the city's prosperity. (Prior to this agreement, Cataluña had been excluded from trading with America; Andalusia, in southern Spain, had been given a monopoly on that particular trade route.) The city's first steam-powered textile factory was opened in 1832, and textile production quickly became the city's leading industry. At one point, the cotton industry alone employed over 80,000 workers. It was a time of rebirth for Barcelona.

The Napoleonic Wars

Once again, war came to Spain, interfering with economic prosperity. This time it was the French ruler Napoleon Bonaparte who forced the Spanish king to give up his throne. He then named his brother, Joseph Bonaparte, king of Spain. The Spanish immediately rebelled, and on May 2, 1808, "el dos de Mayo," the Spanish War of Independence against the French began. A scene from this war is hauntingly depicted in Goya's famous painting, *The Second of May.*

Although the French were well armed, they did not stay long. The Spaniards, joined by British troops, successfully drove them out by 1814, and a monarchy was re-established under Ferdinand VII. The Spanish managed to defeat the French largely because they fought them with a series of hit-and-run battles, called "guerillas" or little wars. The term "guerilla warfare" has been used ever since.

French prisoners are marched into Salamanca during the Napoleonic Wars.

War did not affect Barcelona much, although the pace of life slowed down somewhat. After Napoleon's defeat, however, the economy gained strength. Over the next 50 years, Barcelona became a leading industrial center. People from all over the country went there to find jobs, which were plentiful. Between 1844 and 1853, the city's first railroads were built, joint stock companies were founded, and modern banks were established.

The city's growth and strength were perhaps best symbolized by the fact that the city leaders tore down the massive fortress Philip V had forced upon the people. It had become a hated symbol of repression. In its place, beautiful gardens were planted and the area was named Ciudadela Park. By this time, the population had soared to an all-time high of 1.6 million people.

With such a strong working force, class distinctions became more pronounced. A real upper class formed as well as a distinct middle class. No other city in Spain compared to it.

The site on which Ciudadela Park was built once housed a massive fortress, built during the reign of the hated King Philip V.

Social Unrest: Early Twentieth Century, 1900-1975

By the end of the nineteenth century, Spain's position as an international power was on the decline. The final blow was the loss of its last American colonies—Cuba, Puerto Rico, and the Philippines. Barcelona suffered, too, but less than other cities. Perhaps this was because the city's mayor backed the famous Universal Exposition in 1888. This huge artistic and trade fair created jobs and brought money to the city.

During this period, and into the early 1900s, Spanish political parties and trade unions gained power as the people suffered economic hardship. Control of the government was tossed back and forth between the liberals and conservatives, who supported the economic status quo, and the radicals and trade unions, who wanted reforms.

The workers' revolts and formations of unions during the 1920s in the United States were similar to Barcelona in the early 1900s. During the nineteenth century, the economy had failed to keep up with the rest of Europe and its growing population. This failure led the Spaniards, most notably, the Catalans, to question themselves and their independence. So began a period of uprisings over fair working conditions, fair pay, and other issues related to worker's rights.

Barcelona was the seat of much of this unrest. The city became known as "anarchism's rose of fire."

Continual worker uprisings led to the Tragic Week in 1909, in which more than 60 churches and religious buildings throughout the country were destroyed.

Tranquility returned to Barcelona to some degree during World War I. Since Spain remained neutral throughout the war, Barcelonans sold goods to the various warring nations. But when the war ended, Barcelona's economy collapsed along with the rest of Spain's.

Strikes and violence followed, and a movement for a republican form of government developed among liberals, socialists, and others who no longer wanted a monarchy. In 1931, Barcelonans and most of Spain voted for republican candidates, and King Alfonso XIII fled the country.

Niceto Alcalá Zamora, the first president of the new government, gave more power to the unions and increased wages for farmers and workers. The conservatives, supported by the Catholic Church and the military, were opposed to these reforms. Sparks flew between this right-wing group and the more liberal supporters of the Republic, known as the Loyalists.

By 1934, the country was firmly divided. On the right were the army, monarchists, the Catholic Church, and the fascists. (The fascists supported a military dictatorship.) On the left were the Communists, socialists, trade unions, workers, peasants, and liberals. That year, the socialists joined with Catalan nationalists to lead an uprising against the government. That uprising quickly spread to other parts of

Spain. Although the government put down the revolt, killing over 1,000 people in the process, war seemed inevitable. Violence in the streets became almost an everyday event, with armed bands from both sides brutally dragging opponents from their homes.

The Spanish Civil War

In its simplest form, the Spanish Civil War was a fight for democracy. It officially began in July 1936. The man leading the charge against the new Republic was Generalisimo Francisco Franco. Barcelona, which always represented independence for all, served as headquarters in the battle for democracy.

The battle lines between democracy and fascism were now clearly drawn. German fascists, known as Nazis, and Italian fascists sent troops and planes into Spain to help Franco's cause. In 1937, a German bombing blitz devastated Guernica, a town in the Basque region that had symbolized regional independence for over 400 years. Liberals around the world rallied to defend the Republic. Over 2,800 Americans, many of them journalists and intellectuals, volunteered and formed the Abraham Lincoln Brigade. More than 800 of them were killed in the battle against fascism. The young writer Ernest Hemingway described this great conflict in his novel *For Whom the Bell Tolls*.

DE MADRID
DELEGACION DE PROPAGANDA Y PRENSA

PARRILLA

¡ATACAD!
SOLDADOS DE LA REPUBLICA

The Spanish Civil War pitted the democratically elected republicans against ultra
right-wing elements led by General Francisco Franco.

Under Franco's dictatorship, all demonstrations of Catalonian culture were prohibited. This included dancing the *sardanas,* the symbol of Barcelona's Catalan identity.

The Liberals, with Barcelona as their main center of strength, could not match the strength of Franco and his military troops. The city suffered damage from bombing, and in January 1939, Barcelona surrendered. Generalisimo Francisco Franco was named head of the new government.

So began a dark period for Barcelona. Franco's reign, which was actually a military dictatorship, dissolved the last elements of Cataluñan autonomy. He prohibited all things concerned with Catalan nationalism, such as flying the Cataluñan flag, public use of the Catalan language, and all books written in Catalan. He even abolished the city's native dance, the *sardanas*, long a symbol of Barcelona's heart and soul.

Despite these gloomy times, the spirit of Barcelona was not broken. Catalan nationalism did not die, it simply went underground. And people practiced their language and dance in secret. They had faith that democracy would eventually come and that their city would once again enjoy the freedom it so prized.

The Growth of Democracy

It wasn't until General Franco died in November, 1975, that Spain and Barcelona were able to enjoy a more democratic existence. Under an agreement signed in 1969, Franco named Juan Carlos, grandson of deposed King Alfonso XIII, heir to the throne. Carlos was not allowed to assume power, however, until after Franco's death. Only then could the transition to democracy begin.

Barcelona, in particular, embraced the move toward democracy. One of the most far-reaching changes under Carlos's leadership has been the acceptance of regionalism. Spain started out as a country of many regions (e.g., Castile, Aragon, Cataluña), and in many cities, especially Barcelona, strong regional feelings never lessened. In 1977, over 1 million people demonstrated in Barcelona demanding the passage of an Autonomy Statute that would reinstate the Catalan government. They were successful, and in 1979, the city was granted autonomy. Barcelona was made the capital of the

General Franco ruled Spain under a military dictatorship until 1975.

province of Cataluña. (Cataluña today encompasses the provinces of Barcelona, Gerona, Lerida, and Tarragona.) In Barcelona, the street signs were changed back to Catalan and the language was once again taught in the schools, spoken on radio and TV, and used in many books. But the strength of Cataluñan regionalism is perhaps best symbolized by the return of the *sardanas*. It is performed every Sunday on the plaza of Barcelona's great cathedral, with fellow Barcelonans joining hands to re-enact their ancient dance.

Today, the official title of Cataluña is the "Comunitat Autonoma de Cataluña," known regionally as the Principalitat. Like the United States, with its Republican and Democratic parties, Barcelona, too, has more than one ruling group. Although Cataluña is under right-wing rule, Barcelona has a socialist council led by an independent-minded mayor, Pasqual Maragall.

By allowing Barcelona to exercise its personality and fend for itself, the city—and the rest of Cataluña—has prospered, bringing the whole of Spain into the limelight. Proof in point is Barcelona's role in hosting the Summer Olympics in 1992. It is also the year of the Seville World Fair and the 500th anniversary of Columbus's arrival in America.

Folk dancers perform at Barcelona's International Expo in 1929.

THE PEOPLE

"Any nation that can eat churros and chocolate for breakfast is not required to demonstrate its courage in other ways."
—James Michener

A street artist renders a masterpiece in chalk on a Barcelona sidewalk.

Barcelona is home to many regional theaters such as this one, off La Rambla.

What makes Barcelona unique is its people. Generally speaking, they are a confident lot, filled with pride in their region. It is as if they walk the streets with a strut that boasts, "We are different, special, more aware than the rest of Spain." Through the centuries, in fact, the citizens of Barcelona have forged a reputation for being independent and industrious, while remaining appreciative of the pleasures of life.

Indeed, they are among the most cosmopolitan of the Spaniards, though fiercely proud of their particular history and language. They are known for their pragmatism and common sense (called *seny*), hard work, and great love of music. They have no qualms about bursting into song on the street. Many belong to choral societies and sing in their church choirs, and the younger generation is often enrolled at an early age in clubs that teach the *sardanas*.

In Barcelona, people dance in the street just because they want to. On Sunday morning after mass, dancers gather on the steps of the city's huge Gothic Cathedral. Anyone who wishes can join in the *sardanas*, a group dance in which participants form a ring—as large as necessary to accommodate all dancers. Coats and purses are tossed in the middle and then, with arms raised and hands joined, they dance in complete silence to the repetitive rhythms provided by the *cobla*, a brass band. For some, the *sardanas* is a political gesture, a symbol of solidarity, a rallying point for the expression of regional identity, especially during bad times.

Culture and art are a big part of their lives as well. For a long time, Barcelona has been Spain's most liberal and progressive city—the home of artists Antonio Gaudí, Joan Miró, Salvador Dali, and for a time, Pablo Picasso. It boasts Spain's finest opera house and native Cataluñans such as Pablo Cassals, actor and director Nuria Espert, and opera singer Montserrat Caballe.

Language

Barcelona, as the capital of Cataluña, has two official languages: Catalan and Castilian Spanish, both of which are derived from Latin. Castilian is Spain's official language and what North Americans call Spanish. Catalan, on the other hand, is the special language of the Catalan region. The Catalans take pride in their lilting language, which has been a binding force throughout their history. The Catalan language, they will argue, is not a dialect of Spanish but rather more closely related to southern French Provençal. Many of the city's signs and public notices are in both Catalan and Castilian.

Barcelonans also love to read. Their city is the publishing capital of Spain, with the highest literacy rate in the country. They claim that "there's a bookshop on every corner." Not quite—but there are many to be found.

Vendors sell balloons near the Plaza Cataluña.

La Boqueria is one of Barcelona's most famous markets.

Barcelonans relax in a café in Güell Park.

Barcelona à la Carte: Catalan Food

Barcelonans are renowned for their love of good food, evidenced by the profusion of restaurants and the wide variety of regional dishes. French-style cafés with glass-enclosed terraces and pastry shops similar to those in France, Germany, and Austria offer more creative dishes and desserts than you'll find in the rest of Spain.

Like the country itself, Catalan food has an ancient tradition. In fact, one of the world's oldest cookbooks is Catalan, dating back to the fourteenth century. The cooking draws heavily on the fresh produce of the region and the seafood of the Mediterranean. The variety of dishes ranges from duck with turnips to rabbit in rum, from loin and pig's feet to oven-roasted boar, partridge, and brussel sprouts. The Catalans are most proud of their sausage dishes and various stews.

Pan tomate, slices of bread spread with olive oil and puréed tomatoes, is found in many restaurants, usually eaten as a side dish. Other staples include *zarzuela*, a soup or stew of lobster, crayfish, squid, mussel, and whitefish; *escudella i car d'oll*, a hearty stew of sausage, beans, meatballs, and spices; and *butifarra*, a sausage unique to Cataluña. The famous caramel custard, *crema catalana*, made with eggs, milk, sugar, and cinnamon, is one of Spain's culinary trademarks and one of the world's most popular desserts.

No day, however, is complete without hot chocolate and *churros*, fried dough, usually sprinkled with sugar. Typically, churros are served for breakfast but are also wonderful as an afternoon snack.

One of the best ways to learn about a country—or a city—is to go food shopping. By pretending to be a native you find out how the people really live.

Food stores in Barcelona are quite small: meats, vegetables, fish, spices, and other foods are sold by individual grocers and butchers, rather than in huge supermarkets. And it's all fresh. Because people tend to shop several times a week or even every day, the shopkeepers know what their customers like. The most famous market in Barcelona, La Boqueria, is on La Rambla. Here you can buy a loaf of bread, a whole hog, or a simple sweet.

Eating out in Barcelona is full of surprises, beginning with the hours. The Spanish dine notoriously late. Breakfast tends to be light, consisting of *café con leche* (coffee with hot milk), or hot chocolate, and churros or toast. Lunch, around 2:00 P.M., is usually a large meal and lasts up to two hours. After work, which often lasts until 7:00 or 8:00 P.M., people enjoy *tapas* (snacks) to tide them over until dinner at 10:00 or 11:00 P.M. *Tapas* literally means "lids." They originally consisted of little saucers of snacks served on top of a drink. Today, bars specializing in tapas have platters of delicious tidbits, such as shellfish, slices of omelettes, and vegetables, on display.

A *limpiabota,* or shoeshine boy, keeps busy on a Barcelona street.

Gaudí's mosaic work is vividly displayed at the entrance to Güell Park.

Famous Artists from Barcelona

Antonio Gaudí

Many people say the most compelling reason to visit Barcelona is to see the works of one of the world's most innovative architects, Antonio Gaudí. This Catalan architect is noted for his freedom of form and exuberant style. He was born in a rural part of Cataluña in 1852 and died in Barcelona in 1926. Gaudí, who never married, was completely devoted to architecture. He was also completely devoted to Barcelona. After graduating from the Escuela Provincial de Arquitectura in Barcelona in 1878, he worked almost entirely in or near his beloved city.

Gaudí's buildings are extremely personal in design and feature vivid colors, flowing lines, and curved surfaces. He made building look so easy; he molded stone into flowing elements of nature and spun wrought iron into whimsical and decorative patterns. His early work, in particular, shows the influence of colorful tiles, used by the Moors in their buildings over 1,000 years ago. Gaudí's Casa Vicens, finished in 1880, began a modern revival of tile in architecture.

Among his most intriguing works are two houses done in the early 1900s, the Casa Mila and Casa Batlló, and an exotic hillside park called the Park Güell. His most famous structure is the unfinished Church of the Sagrada Familia.

Left: A lamppost believed to be designed by Gaudí stands in a small plaza off La Rambla. *Below:* The Casa Mila apartment building, which has no straight walls, is a good illustration of Gaudí's use of organic forms. *Right:* A closer look at a chimney from the roof of the Casa Mila apartments.

Although Gaudí was regarded as eccentric, he was also much admired and considered an important contributor to the Catalan "Renaixensa," an artistic and political revival that aimed to bring back an independent Cataluña. The religious symbol of this movement was Gaudí's church, the Sagrada Familia, which was commissioned in 1883. Its tall, pointy spires and its "cave-like" exterior are a striking and unique sight. The longer Gaudí worked on this project the more religious he became. After 1910, he abandoned all other assignments and began living on the site in his workshop. At the age of 75, on his way to vespers, Gaudí was hit by a trolly car and died. Work on the church, which has become the unofficial symbol of Barcelona, is still ongoing. No one knows when, or even if, this wonderful structure will ever be finished.

José Louis Sert

This architect, noted for his humanistic approach to city planning and urban development, was born outside Barcelona in 1902 and died there in 1983. After graduating from the Escuela Superior d'Arquitectura in Barcelona in 1929, Sert worked with Le Corbusier in Paris. From 1929 to 1937, he had his own architectural firm in Barcelona where he designed a number of apartment houses as well as a master plan for the city.

In 1939, Sert moved to the United States and became a partner in a New York architectural firm. His designs for such cities as Rio de Janeiro and Bogotá are still studied today. In his later years, Sert devoted much of his time to teaching others. As the dean of the Graduate School of Design at Harvard University, he influenced several generations of city planners.

Sert's most famous work in Barcelona is the Joan Miró Foundation, finished in 1975. It houses works by his friend and fellow Barcelona native, Joan Miró.

Joan Miró

This Catalan artist, a leader in abstract art and surrealist fantasy, was born in Barcelona in 1893. He died in Majorca in 1983. If it had been up to Miró's parents, he would never have become an artist. They insisted he attend a regular high school rather than art school. He failed to graduate, however, and instead attended a commercial school and worked two years as an office clerk. He became increasingly despondent and eventually suffered a mental collapse. After recovering, Miró's parents granted him his wish—to attend art school in Barcelona. His teacher, Francisco Gali, introduced him to the fantastic world of Gaudí, an influence that would change his life.

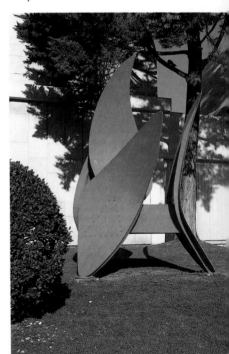

Artist Joan Miró is known for his paintings and playful, abstract sculptures.

From 1915 to 1919, Miró worked in Barcelona painting landscapes and portraits. After 1919, he divided his time between Spain and Paris, using both as subjects for his mysterious, dream-like paintings. By the 1930s, his art included decor designs for ballets and tapestries. A favorite technique was to spill paint on the canvas and move his brush around in it. During this time he was also active in a variety of mediums: collage, murals, book illustrations, sculpture, and ceramics.

During the Spanish Civil War, Miró's works mirrored the terrors and horrors of his homeland's political turmoil. *The Reaper* stands out as strong social criticism of the era.

After the war, Miró became world famous for his paintings, pottery, sculpture, and beautiful book illustrations. Totally unaffected by his fame, he continued to devote himself to observing and creating, to putting his special inner vision into art for others to both question and enjoy.

Salvador Dali

Dream-like paintings and unique drawings were also the domain of Catalan Salvador Dali (1904–1989). Dali was, more than the other artists of this period, concerned with creating his own vision of a fantasy world. He was particularly interested in the inner workings of the mind, and his works often showed wholly unrelated objects grouped together.

Surrealist artist Salvador Dali loved to shock the public with his grand gestures and eccentric behavior.

He illustrated books, some of them his own texts, and also worked on films. In his later years, he began painting a number of religious objects.

Many consider Dali not only eccentric—"off the wall," really—but a great self-promoter.

Although Dali was born in Cataluña, there has always been a great rivalry between Madrid and Barcelona as to where his allegiances were. In the end, Madrid and Barcelona divided up the bulk of his works, which he had left upon his death to the Spanish Culture Ministry.

ON THE TOUR BUS

Landmarks

Ajuntamiento de Barcelona (Town Hall), Plaza de Sant Jaume. Restored to its original glory, it is easy to imagine Barcelona's ancestors arguing over politics in this ancient Gothic building.

La Barceloneta. Built in 1755, this area was traditionally the home of workers and fishermen. Come at lunchtime to its main thoroughfares, the Paseo Nacional or Moll de la Barceloneta, and feast on fresh seafood in no-frills restaurants.

El Barrio Gótico, central Barcelona. Otherwise known as the Gothic Quarter and formerly called "the Cathedral Quarter." It is here where the principal Gothic buildings, marking the high point of the Middle Ages, as well as remnants of Roman times can be found. The best way to explore the area is to walk its cobblestoned streets; each corner holds a surprise.

Casa Mila, in the Ensanche, 92 Paseo de Gracia. Also known as La Pedrera, this Gaudí-designed apartment house features intricate ironwork and egg-shaped windowpanes. The roof terrace is the most famous, with strange formations covering the chimneys and ventilators.

El Call. In the Middle Ages, Barcelona's Jewish quarter, called *El Call* in Catalan, lay to the west of Carrer Bisbe and Plaza de Sant Jaume. Today, the area has many antique shops and ancient streets. Walk along Carrer de la Palla and Banys Nous for some of the most interesting sites.

La Rambla. The city's liveliest pedestrian promenade runs from the huge square at Plaza de Cataluña down to the sea. The Plaza, an open space surrounded by tall shade trees, is the focal point for the city's major celebrations.

Olympic Ring, Montjuïc. The sports facilities that, on July 20-August 9, 1992, are the site of the Summer Olympics.

Parque Güell, on Calle Larrad in the Ensanche. Originally

A mosaic lizard in Güell Park

planned by Gaudí and his friends as a garden city, the project failed. But today it contains two gingerbread-type houses in a beautiful park. Gaudí built the houses by hand, putting together rocks, colorful tiles, and pieces of old glass to create a whimsical setting. Inexpensive lunches and drinks are served outside overlooking terraced gardens.

Palacio de la Generalidad (Statehouse, on Plaza de Sant Jaume). A fifteenth-century Gothic structure that once housed the ancient Cataluñan parliament and today is the site of the executive branch of Cataluña's autonomous government.

Palacio Real (Great Royal Palace), in the Gothic Quarter, on the Plaza del Rey. The former fourteenth-century palace of the Counts of Barcelona. Legend has it that the Catholic Monarchs welcomed Columbus here upon his return from the New World.

Pueblo Español (Spanish Village), Avenida Margues de Comillas, on Montjuïc. Built for the 1929 World's Fair, this reconstructed "village" set on five acres contains exhibits of Spanish art and architecture.

Tibidabo Mountain. The best view of the city is from the top

The Casa Batlló, designed by Gaudí, on the Paseo de Gracia

of Tibidabo; summit reached by car, cab, or bus.

The Waterfront. The area that gave the city its longstanding seafaring traditions. Today, you'll see cruise ships here as well as Columbus's statue, El Monumento a Colón, erected in 1886. It is the tallest monument honoring the explorer in the world. Take the elevator to the top floor for a great view of the city. Also nearby is *The Maritime Museum,* parts of which date

back to the thirteenth century, and the *Santa Maria,* a full-scale reproduction of the ship on which Columbus sailed to America.

Markets

Antiques Market. Held in the square in front of the Gothic Cathedral on Thursday mornings. *Artists Market.* Paintings and crafts; held on Saturday mornings in the Placeta del Pi. *Boqueria Market.* A typical and colorful food market on La Rambla between Carme and Hospital. It fills a huge 1914 vaulted iron and glass arcade; open Mondays through Saturdays. *El Encants.* Barcelona's giant flea market, held on Mondays, Wednesdays, Fridays, and Saturdays, at the end of El Dos de Mayo on the Plaza Glories Catalanes. *San Antonio Market.* Collections of second-hand books, old magazines, postcards, press cuttings, and prints. Held on Sunday mornings in the old market building at the corner of Urgell and Tamarit at the end of Ronda Sant Antoni. *Stamp and Coin Market.* Held on Sunday mornings in the Plaza Real, a neoclassical square that dates back to 1848. The decorative lampposts are said to be designed by Gaudí.

Museums

Frederic Mares Museum, 10 Carrera del Comtes de Barcelona, Gothic Quarter. Offered to the city by the sculptor Frederic Mares, the museum is crammed with Roman relics and sculptures from the Middle Ages.

La Fundación Miró (Joan Miró Foundation), on Montjuïc. The best works of this surrealist painter and sculptor are here. The building, designed by Miró's friend Sert, was opened in 1975.

An Art Nouveau storefront on a street by La Rambla

Barcelona's unusual hearse museum

Museo de Historia de la Ciudad (Museum of City History), Plaza del Rey, Gothic Quarter. Connected to the Palacio Real, this museum contains examples of the city's history from its days as a Carthaginian trading port. Begin with the Roman ruins and baths located underground and work your way up, floor by floor, century by century.

Museo de Arte de Cataluña (Museum of Cataluñan Art), on Montjuïc. Known as the "Prado of Romanesque Painting," it is housed inside the impressive National Palace, built for the 1929 World's Fair. Gothic works as well as canvases by some of Spain's greatest painters are here.

Museo Arquelógico (Archaeological Museum), on Carrera de Lérida, on Montjuïc. Exhibits showing Spain's prehistoric relics as well as artifacts of the Greeks, Romans, and Carthaginians.

Museo Picasso, on Carrera de Montcada, near Pincesa. Hundreds of canvases, painted by the young artist between 1896 and 1917, show the development of the founder of Cubism and remind us that he wasn't always a modernist. His earliest drawings, done as a child, are grouped together in the first gallery.

Museo del Futbol Club de Barcelona (Barcelona Soccer Museum), Camp Nou Stadium. Trophies and videos highlighting the club's famous history.

Churches

La Catedral, on Carrer de Santa Llucia in the Gothic Quarter. Otherwise known as "The Cathedral," it was built on the site of a Romanesque church in the late thirteenth century. The bells ring every quarter hour. Toward the southern end is a lively area called the Cloister, where street musicians entertain those walking by. A small museum in the Chapterhouse contains various religious treasures.

La Sagrada Familia (Church of the Holy Family), Plaza de la Sagrada Familia in the Ensanche. This is Antonio Gaudí's famous unfinished work and the unofficial symbol of the city. It was begun in 1883 and is still incomplete. The church is arranged in the shape of the Latin cross.

Pedralbes Monastery, at Tibidabo. A group of fourteenth-century buildings that include a single-aisle church and three-story cloister.

San Pedro de las Puellas, Plaza de San Pedro. Supposedly the oldest church in Barcelona, dating to the early 800s.

Parks and Zoos

Parque de la Ciudadela (Citadel Park). The citadel, a massive military fortress built in 1716, was pulled down in the late 1860s and replaced with public gardens. In the park are the Geology and Natural History Museums, the Museum of Modern Art, a zoo, aquarium, and the Catalan Regional Parliament.

The northern façade of the Sagrada Familia cathedral

Feeding the swans in the Ciudadela Park

Parque Güell, in the northwest part of the city. Begun by Gaudí, this park is full of Art Nouveau works. Not only does it offer Gaudí's incredible mosaics but also postcard-perfect views.

Parque de Montjuïc. Its name, most historians agree, means "Mountain of the Jews," from the time when much of Barcelona's Jewish population was buried there. The gardens surrounding the hill were laid out for the International Exhibition in 1929. You'll get a splendid view over the city.

Parque Zoológico, at La Ciudadela. The larger African animals are a sight to see; many are shown in their natural surroundings.

Events

On January 5, the splendid *Calvacade of the Three Kings* (or Three Wise Men) takes place. That evening, children put out their shoes. When they wake up on the morning of the 6th, they find them filled with presents.

On January 17, or the closest Sunday, the *Els Tres Tombs* parade of horses takes place. This ceremony dates back to the fifteenth century. The horses are blessed by their patron saint, Saint Anthony Abbot. The term *three* is used because the rider turns his animal around three times as it is being blessed. Some Barcelonans take their dogs and other pets, dressed with colored ribbons to be blessed. On this day, "tortells de Sant Antoni" are eaten—marzipan cake with little porcelain animals inside as surprises.

The *Festivity of Saint Eulalia*, the original patron of the city, includes a number of events in February with a medieval flavor, including plays, dances, and parades made up of giant figures.

In late February or early March, the *International Vintage*

Because Barcelonans take their food seriously, the city abounds with many fine restaurants.

Car Rally takes place, running from Barcelona to Sitges.

On March 3, the popular *Festival of Saint Medir* is held with a parade of horses, carriages, lorries, and cars. Onlookers are showered with sweets. All participants wear a rosary made from beans, a plant that recalls the legend of the saint.

On *Easter Sunday*, groups of young people dressed in old Cataluñan costumes, sing "caramellas" (songs wishing joy and good health) in the city's squares.

On *Whit Sunday* in La Barceloneta, the seaman's district, two processions take place. In the first one, each person wears a decorated tool (axe, knife, fork, etc.), symbolizing the utensils for eating or the tools of their trade. On the return procession, they carry home food—chickens, sausage, rabbits, etc.—for their families.

The year's most spectacular festival takes place on April 23, when Cataluña's patron saint, *Saint George*, is honored. People build human towers by standing on each other's backs in pyramid fashion that sometimes reach as high as eight men. This festival coincides with The Day of the Book and Rose Day. In 1923, the publishers' association instituted Book Day, when new editions in Catalan were presented. The festival ceased after the Civil War but began again in the fifties. It is customary to give a book and a rose as a present symbolizing friendship and love.

On May 11, the *Festival of Saint Ponc* held on El Hospital street. Herbs, medicinal plants, honey and candied fruit of ancient origin are displayed.

From June 23-24, bonfires and fireworks celebrate the *summer solstice*. People save their old furniture and other material for several weeks in anticipation of the fires. A dance is held on Montjuïc.

At the end of June and during the month of July, theatre, dancing, flamenco, classical, and contemporary music concerts are held in connection with the *Greek Festival*. These take place either in the Greek Theatre in Montjuïc or outdoors.

Around the *Feast of the Assumption* (August 15th) parades are held.

September 11 is *Catalan National Day*. It marks the defeat of the Catalan government and the fall of its capital, Barcelona, on September 11, 1714, into the hands of Philip V. The day has always symbolized national resistance and was secretly celebrated during the

The park on Montjuïc, just below the Olympic Stadium

Franco years. Since his death, it has been openly proclaimed by hanging the *senyera* (Catalan flag) from walls, balconies, windows, and shopfronts.

September 24 is the *Festival of Our Lady of Mercy*, patron saint of the city. Typical dances, such as the *sardanas*, parades, and sporting events (sailing, regattas, swimming, and walking races), take place.

B.C.

ca. 100,000 B.C. Iberians inhabit the area that is today Barcelona.

ca. 400 B.C. Carthaginians, from Africa, conquer the region.

281 B.C. Hamilcar Barca, a member of Carthage's ruling family, names the city "Barcino," after himself.

A.D.

ca. 100 B.C.–
A.D. 406 Roman rule flourishes in Barcelona; commerce grows; laws are established; bridges, roads, and aqueducts are constructed.

415–711 Germanic Christian Visigoths conquer the city; Ataulfo makes Barcelona the capital of the Visigoth Kingdom.

711 Moors attack and easily defeat the Visigoths.

718–756 Moors rule the region, many people become Muslims.

800s–1100s Barcelona is ruled by a series of counts.

1200s King James I creates the municipality of Barcelona.

1400s–1600s Ferdinand and Isabella, the "Catholic Monarchs," rule the region and institute the Spanish Inquisition; they also send explorer Christopher Columbus on a journey to the New World in 1492. In 1519, Charles V reigns.

1640 War of the Harvesters begins, started by middle class workers who revolted against French rule, which lasted until 1653.

1653 After defeating the French, Barcelona goes back to Spanish rule.

1701 War of Spanish Succession begins, fought over who was to inherit the throne. Philip V of Spain won the war and captured Barcelona with the rest of Spain.

1808 Spanish War of Independence is fought against France's Napolean Bonaparte.

1814 French are driven out and the monarchy is reestablished under Ferdinand VII.

1832 The first steam-powered textile factory opens, beginning a new era of industry for the city.

1844–1853	First railroads are built; Ciudadela is built.
1888–1899	Barcelona hosts the Universal Exposition; Spain loses its last American colonies—Cuba, Puerto Rico, and the Philippines.
1900–1930	Political parties and trade unions gain power; government goes back and forth between liberals and conservatives, radicals and trade unions; Spain remains neutral during World War I (1914–1918).
1931	Republican candidates who want to abolish the monarchy win the elections; King Alfonso XIII flees the country and Niceto Zamora becomes the first president of the Republic.
1934	Spain is divided between the army's pro-monarchist fascists, and the liberal peasant workers who favor the Republic.
1936–1939	The Spanish Civil War rages across Spain; the war is a fight between the fascists, led by Francisco Franco, and the Loyalists, who favor the Republic; General Franco is named the new head of the government in 1939.
1939–1975	Franco outlaws all elements of Barcelona's autonomy and individual culture until his death in 1975.
1975	Juan Carlos, grandson of Alfonso XIII, takes the throne and begins a transition to democracy.
1979	The Catalan government is reinstated and granted full autonomy; Barcelona is made the capital of the region.
1980s	Catalan nationalism and culture experiences a rebirth.
1992	Barcelona is host to the Summer Olympics and celebrates the 500th anniversary of Columbus's journey to America.

For Further Reading

Barcelona (Everything Under the Sun Travel Guide Series). National Textbook Co., 1987.
Spain (Cadogan Guides). Globe Pequot Press, 1989.
Birnbaum's Spain/Portugal (Stephen Birnbaum Travel Guides). Houghton Mifflin, 1989.
James Michener. *Iberia*.
Jan Morris. *Spain*.
Miguel de Cervantes. *Don Quixote*.
Ernest Hemingway. *The Sun Also Rises*.
Washington Irving. *Tales of the Alhambra*.
George Orwell. *Homages to Cataluña*.

Where to Get More Information

For general travel and tourist brochures, contact the nearest Tourist Office of Spain:

Chicago
845 North Michigan Avenue
Chicago, IL 60611
312–642-1992

Los Angeles
San Vicente Plaza Building
Suite 960
8383 Wilshire Boulevard
Beverly Hills, CA 90211
213–658-7188

Miami
Suite 185
1221 Brickell Avenue
Miami, FL 33131
305–358-1992

New York
665 Fifth Avenue
New York, NY 10022
212–759-8822

Toronto
60 Bloor Street West
201, Toronto, Ontario M4W3B8
416–961-3131

For information on traveling to Barcelona, contact: IBERIA, the Spanish National Airline, which has offices in major cities.

For information on cultural matters, contact:
The Education Office of the Consulate of Spain
150 Fifth Avenue
New York, NY 10011
212–741-5144

For information on commercial matters, contact:
Commercial Office of Spain
405 Lexington Avenue
New York, NY 10017
212–661-4959

INDEX

Photo credits
Cover, pages 4–5, 8–9, 10, 11, 12–13 (all), 15, 16, 23, 33, 38, 42–43, 44, 46 (top and bottom), 47, 48, 49 (all), 51, 54, 55, 56 (bottom left), 57, 58 (left), 59, © Richard Glassman; p. 18–19, 32, Photosearch; p. 22, 25, 27, 41, Institut Museu D'Historia, Barcelona; p. 39, 53, UPI/Bettmann Newsphotos; p. 56 (top right), Institut Municipal Dels Serveis Funeraris, Barcelona; p. 59 (bottom), © Danilo Boschung/Leo de Wys, Inc. Map by Robert Italiano.